LOVE CONQUERS ALL

D.L. SMITH

STRATTON
PRESS
Publishing Life

LOVE CONQUERS ALL

Stratton Press Publishing
831 N Tatnall Street Suite M #188,
Wilmington, DE 19801
www.stratton-press.com
1-888-323-7009

ISBN (Paperback): 978-1-64895-596-9
ISBN (Ebook): 978-1-64895-597-6

Printed in the United States of America

CHAPTER I

The Wedding

"Dearly beloved, we are gathered here to join in the holy bonds of matrimony—" as Julia heard the minister pronouncing the cliché words for the same way they had been pronounced for hundreds of years on and on, she stood motionless in a sea of wonderment. What strange surroundings for a girl who had led the life she had been unfortunate enough to fall into, like a steel trap. It had always seemed that she felt herself falling as if she had no choice, and yet she was always grasping for the few wonderful moments of life that she thought she should be entitled to. After all, she was born into this world for some reason. What it was, she had never been able to find out.

CHAPTER II

EARLY CHILDHOOD

At one time back in her early childhood, she had thought it might be that she was only here to upset and disappoint her mother. After all, when her mother constantly told her how disappointed in her she was, what would a child of eight think? Like the time she had pushed her little brother down because she was angry at him for being the one getting all her mother's attention. She could still remember every word bitterly etched into her mind as if it has been branded there with the fire of hate, sizzling with bitterness.

"Julia, what in heaven's name are you doing? Answer me. Why did you push Jimmy down like that? You're just plain mean. Honestly Julia, sometimes you disappoint me so that I don't know why you were born. Come here, Jimmy, let mother see."

Julia had always been an introvert and every time her mother made a remark like this, she just looked with that hate-filled blank expression as if she were staring right straight through everyone and everything into the depth of hell. Nothing or nobody was going to stop her if she wanted to do something, and no amount of punishment would prevent her from doing it again if she wanted to.

"Now, young lady, if I ever see you do that again, so help me, I'll take Papa's belt and wear it out on you. You ought to be ashamed. A helpless little one-year-old baby, and you push him down like he is a kid your own age. Now you go into your room, and stay and think about it a little while. While you're at it, ask the Lord what in heaven's name he sent you into this world for, anyway. I can't seem to make you want to do one decent thing. And that blank face of yours. I wonder what devil's work you're cooking up in that brain of yours. Oh, you've got a good brain, alright. Maybe, too good. You're so smart you can think of things that an ordinary eight-year-old-girl shouldn't even be able to read. Now, go!"

As Julia walked to her room and quietly shut the door (After all, slamming it wouldn't do any good; just make her mother say the same things over and over), she sat down on her bed and began to dream of a beautiful life. She'd get out of this place and make people notice her, and she'd be the favorite of everybody who was rich and famous and somebody. Now she would just dream away the time until Mama came to the door and asked her if she was ready to come out. She didn't really mind being sent to her room at all, In fact, she enjoyed the quiet, dark room all by herself. At least, Jimmy couldn't bother her in here. Mama probably sent her in here so she could watch Jimmy and not have to see her, too, because she was a bitter disappointment to Mama. She knew she was. She had red hair and freckles, and her mouth was too big and her legs were knobby, and Jimmy was such a beautiful baby, with curly brown hair like Mama's, and large almond-shaped eyes and long lashes, and he was so cute and plump. Julia secretly thought that her mother hated her because she looked like her father, and she could never see that they seemed to love one another. There was never a word of love or soft touches such as she had seen in the movies when she would go with Carla. She loved Carla because she would take her to the movies and buy her popcorn, and they would talk about so many things. Carla was fourteen and an only child. Julia envied her for that. At least, she didn't have to watch where she put things so they wouldn't be broken nor watch how quietly she shut doors as not to awaken the baby.

CHAPTER III

Memories Flood In

"The ring is the symbol of unending love, undying devotion to one whom God has given." Strange that she should be here. She really didn't love the one beside her with undying devotion. He knew that, but he still loved her and asked her to marry him. She had to get hold of herself. She had almost laughed out loud when she thought of the day, so long ago, so many heartbreaks ago when she had been asked to marry Greg. She was only fifteen, and yet she could still laugh about it.

"Julia, I know we're just fifteen, but promise me that you won't go out with anybody else and that you'll marry me when we got out of school."

"That's silly. Of course, I'll go out with anyone else who asks me. You don't own me, you know. Just because you come over to the house all the time and take my little brother riding on your bike and we go fishing together

all the time, that doesn't mean you own me at all. So just get that out of your head right now."

"You'd probably go out with anybody who asks you just to get away from your mother, wouldn't you? I know how you feel about her and your father and about Jimmy, too. I can tell that you hate that kid with a genuine hate that I haven't ever seen in anyone else. You know that kid loves you, and you treat him like a dog. Why, Julia? Why do you hate that kid so much?"

"What I do say and how I feel about my family is my own business. You just mind yours, and we can still go fishing together and all, but I'm getting out of here someday and I'm going to meet someone who's going to take care of me and buy me things, and he's going to do anything for me to make me happy and love just me. Nobody else, just me."

"You're selfish, you know that? You're the oldest girl I know. Do you think that the whole world ought to revolve around just you? Well, it won't ever, and the quicker you come to that conclusion the quicker you're going to be happy. That's always been your problem. You hate Jimmy because he requires attention, and you think you ought to get it all. What do you think you are anyhow, some kind of princess of something?"

"You just wait, you'll see. You think you're smart. You must be off your rocker thinking I'd marry you. I'm going to marry somebody.

"And what do you think I am, dirt under your feet or something, your highness? Please, forgive me." As he mockingly bowed with a sweep of his hand, Julia kicked him and he fell backward into the river. She ran home

and into her bedroom and locked the door. She was afraid he might come after her, but for the life of her, she couldn't get the look out of her mind and she buried her face into her pillow and laughed until she cried.

CHAPTER IV
The Graduation

She noticed that the minister had a quizzical look on his face as he glanced at her, and she felt that she had been smiling a little too much. She replaced the smile with a very solemn look, and dared not look at Greg or she would laugh out loud.

Suddenly, she remembered their graduation. Their auditorium was filled with doting parents and grandparents, old friends and neighbors, townspeople and dignitaries, all seemingly proud of the young graduates, full of congratulations and good wishes for the future. As she was shaking hands and smiling at first one and the other, suddenly she looked up and there was someone she didn't know. His face was suntanned, his hand was rugged as if he had been accustomed to hard work, and his smile was startling. She couldn't help staring for a few seconds, and then whip, she realized they were standing there holding hands as if everyone else had mysteriously vanished and they were all alone. She managed to stammer a "Thank you very much" and faint smile. He released her hand rather reluctantly, and there followed some small talk which neither of them could remember later. That night in the dark stillness of her bedroom, she thought about him and dreamed wildly about him. That alarmingly steady gaze and his smile, they were something to dream about. She could envision many romantic moments with this man. He was old enough to be her father. He was dark, mysterious, ruggedly handsome stranger who came from nowhere to fill her mind with wonderful dreams. She finally went to sleep sometime in the early hours of morning, and when she awoke, she should have been tired since she must have just gotten three or four hours of sleep at the most. But, as if magically rested by some unknown herb or secret not known to man, she awoke and fervently dressed. She had such a desire to get out and walk, going nowhere in particular but everywhere. After all, she was free now. She had her high school diploma in her bedroom, she was seventeen now, and ready to get out of this place.

She started out toward the river—the familiar place where she and Greg had spent so many hours fishing, swimming, and just sitting under the big shade trees and looking upward at the clouds drifting lazily by like giant puffs of white steam. As she crossed the road, she noticed a car coming toward her. And just as she was about to step over the ditch to take the path toward the river, she heard her name. As she looked back, she dared not believe what she saw. There in a dark green convertible with his arm draped over the door as if he was resting from a hard day's work flashing that disarming smile of his, was the stranger from yesterday.

"Your name is Julia, isn't it?"

"Yes, but how'd you know?"

"Well, I just asked one of the kids who you graduated with yesterday who the redhead was, and he told me. Is that simple enough?"

"I guess so." He seemed to be just watching her as you'd sit and watch a movie or a play. He kept the warm smile, and his dark eyes seemed to be smiling, too. There was something so friendly about his whole countenance that she couldn't resist walking toward the car.

"My name is Art Runyon. I never did get around to introducing myself yesterday. We just seemed to shake hands and that was all."

She smiled because she remembered how they had stood staring into each other's eyes, completely oblivious to everyone around them.

"Were you going anywhere in particular?"

"No, not really. Just down to the river, maybe, Just to kill time."

"Now that's something you should never kill. Time is something very important. When you get as old as I am, you'll realize how important it really is."

"You're not old."

"Oh yes, I am, Julia. I don't lie about my age to myself or to anyone else. I hope you never will, either. If you do everything you want to do while you're using your time, then you won't ever regret any of it enough that you'll want to lie about how much time you've used."

"I guess, I just hadn't ever thought about it one way or the other."

"Well, you should. Now you've graduated, you have to begin thinking how you intend to spend all that time that you've been allotted. Right now, I wish you'd spend a little of it showing me around the country. I've never been here before, and I'd like to see some of it before I go back tomorrow."

"Why are you here, anyway? I don't ever remember seeing you before."

"You haven't. I came here for the graduation. James Little is my nephew. My namesake, too, and he asked me to come. He's the one who told me your name."

"But you said name was Art."

"James Arthur Runyon, ma'am. At your service." He pretended to bow, and when he did, he hit his head on the steering wheel and uttered some kind of profanities under his breath. It was the first time she had seen him without that wonderful smile on his face, and it suddenly was funny to her. When she giggled, he reached out and caught her and playfully pretended to reach down and spank her. As he did reach over the door, his arm rested on her breast, and suddenly, she didn't know how it happened. He was holding her as if he could squeeze the breath out of her, but it was so tender, so warm that she relaxed. She didn't know how long he held her, but when he let her go, she didn't move. She was standing as if she were out of breath. Her heart was pounding so that she could hardly hear when he said, "Get in."

CHAPTER V
THE NEW BEGINNING

She sat on the far side of the seat, leaning against the door and staring at him. She had no idea where he was driving to nor did the she care. She had never felt this way about anyone. There was that time last year down by the river when Greg had quietly leaned over her and caressed her breasts and put his hands inside her sweater, and she had enjoyed that. She knew she shouldn't have but the feeling was, and there wasn't any use in wishing it weren't. She just leaned back and let him unhook her bra and play with her breast. It felt good, and she was sure that if Jimmy hadn't come down the path looking for her, she would have let Greg unbutton her slacks and go all the way. But there was Jimmy, screaming his head off for her, and it was all they could do to get her bra hooked and sweater down it time.

Now, she looked at Art looking straight ahead as if he wasn't even aware that she was in the car. She studied his face, his hands. He had a scar, a small one, on his cheek in front of his ear. She wondered who or what was responsible for that. His eyes looked like cold embers when they were looking away, but once he turned to her, those eyes were like magnifying glasses looking into her very soul. She felt a stirring in her stomach—fright or anticipation, she didn't know which. She also felt other stirrings lower down, and she didn't know whether to be afraid or happy that she could feel this way. She had once decided that she wasn't capable of passion since she wasn't sure she was capable of love. She had never particularly been a loving person. She didn't love Jimmy, that was for sure. She didn't even know whether she loved her parents or not. She had wondered if she would ever be able to love anyone with the same feeling that her girlfriends had when they said they loved various boys. They had also told her about passion, too, and many of them had described in detail how they felt when they went *all the way* as they said.

She hadn't ever felt anything like this with Greg. After all, he was the only one she was ever around, so how could she judge how girls were supposed to feel? Once, when Carla had taken her to a movie and met her boyfriend there and when they thought she was watching the movie, she noticed he put his hand under Carla's skirt and his other hand under her blouse and she heard Carla's breathing get deeper. Julia pretended to be very intent on watching the movie, but out of the corner of her eye, she saw how she reached over to his pants and slowly unzipped them and slid her hand through the zipper. At that time, Julie had noticed that she felt little ripples of what she had later decided was passion. At least it was sexual desire, even if it was someone else's. She felt it, and that meant she was human, anyway.

Finally, the car stopped. She looked out to see where they were and was surprised to see that they were overlooking the river. She recognized this place since her family had come here to picnics a few times. It was about twenty miles from where she lived. She was surprised that they had gotten there so quickly, or at least it seemed quickly. When she turned toward him, she noticed he had slid out from under the wheel and was closer to her. He leaned over and kissed her. "Julia, I—" He stopped short, without words to say what he wants to.

"What were you going to say?"

"I don't really know. All I know is that I feel something for you I've never felt for anyone before. Julia, do you know that you're what, seventeen?" She nodded her head and never took her eyes off his mouth. "Well, I'm forty. Do you know what that means? I'm old enough to be your father. You shouldn't even be here with me. You know that, don't you?" She nodded her head again, and suddenly she had a wild desire to be kissed by that mouth again. That beautiful, smiling mouth with the teeth that looked whiter since the face was so tanned. She felt herself moving toward him. She couldn't have stopped if she wanted to. Then they were in each other's arms, just holding one another tightly, kissing each other with open desire. She suddenly was frightened and pulled away. This was something new to her. She sat rigidly on the edge of the seat and even felt as if she was going to cry.

"Julia, my little, Julia. I won't hurt you. I'll never do anything to you unless you want me to. I promise you, I won't. Please, don't be afraid of me. Or are you afraid of yourself? Have you ever been loved? Really loved?"

"No." She felt the tears running down her cheeks and she felt ashamed. Ashamed for her feelings of guilt, and embarrassed, too, because she was crying. She couldn't stop them. Then he held her, caressing her hair and her cheeks, kissing her face lightly, her lips, her neck. She didn't know how long it was until she was calm, tears gone, wiped clean with his handkerchief. They just sat there quietly, watching each other, holding hands. She felt something she had never known before. She knew this was love. She felt it with every muscle in her body.

"Will you please take me home now?" She knew it was getting late, and she didn't want to give her parents anything to accuse her of or shout at her about. This was one night she wanted to feel at peace and dream the dreams of one in love. She didn't even know if this man was married and didn't care. All she knew was that she was madly in love. Next time, she would give him herself and have all the love there was to have. The love of feeling another close without clothes, without being afraid. She knew when he asked her, she would say yes.

He drove her back to the road where he had first seen her and stopped the car. Reaching for her hand, he kissed her palm, then leaned over and kissed her lightly on the lips. “I’ll see you here tomorrow morning at the same time, okay?”

She shook her head yes, got out of the car, and ran down the trail. She wanted to sit and think a few minutes before she went home. She heard the car start, then drive away. She didn’t look back but kept running toward the trees and her familiar surroundings. When she got to the friendly shade, she sat down as if she had been running for miles and miles without resting. She suddenly felt so tired that she couldn’t stand to think of even walking home, yet she had a satisfied feeling about her, a new feeling—the feeling of loving and being loved.

The next morning, she was awake at dawn but she couldn’t get dressed because she knew that would arouse her mother’s suspicious nature. So she just lay in bed, dreaming of Art. There were so many things she wanted to know about him, and yet all she wanted to know right now was that she loved him and he loved her. She knew he did because of the look he gave her when he asked her to meet him today. She wasn’t very familiar with love except in the movies, but she knew that was love. She also knew what would happen that day, too. She didn’t know how it would feel or how everything would look, but she knew what would happen. Then, she suddenly sat straight up in as if startled out of a deep sleep. She had a sudden, terrifying thought that if she did that, she would surely get pregnant and she didn't want that to happen to her. Carla had gotten pregnant, and it was such a disgrace—all the gossip, and her mother telling everyone that Carla had tuberculosis and had to go away for a while for a rest. Nobody believed her because Carla had begun to show before her mother had suspicioned anything was wrong. Carla had told her about it. She had met the day after Easter with her boyfriend from the movies, and they had spent the whole day in a motel while her mother worked. Carla had told her mother that she was spending the day with a girlfriend and that they had gone to the library most of the day, and her mother had believed her. Then, when school dismissed for summer and Carla knew she was pregnant, she would have him come to the house right after her mother went to work and they would have all day long to be naked if they wanted to, or go to bed, or whatever they wanted to do. Carla had told her it was almost like being married. Then the whole thing exploded one day when Carla's mother saw her pulling clothes off to take a bath. It was so very evident that she was pregnant, and Carla broke down and told her the whole story. It was awful. Julia didn't want that for herself.

After thinking a couple of hours, she decided to take her bath and get dressed. She chose her prettiest lingerie, her sexiest jersey pullover blouse and a pair of white shorts. She also used a lot of cologne that she had gotten for graduation from her aunt in Chicago. She felt very feminine and alluring. At least, she did before she went downstairs.

"Julia, I'm going into town this morning and I want you to look after the house and Jimmy while I'm gone."

"But I can't," she fairly screamed it before she caught herself. She realized she had done the wrong thing when her mother looked at her suspiciously.

"Why can't you? What else have you got to do?"

"I promised a friend that I'd meet him at the Titans library this morning, and then go for a hamburger and malt. I don't want to stay here with that little brat. He's big enough to look after himself now, anyway."

"You sure it's just a friend? Is it Greg? You've always seen a whole lot of that boy, and sometimes I don't particularly like those long hours you spend on the river."

"No. it isn't Greg. Besides, I'm old enough to pick my friends now. After all, I graduated, and now I'm thinking about going somewhere and getting a job and being on my own. I certainly don't intend to stay around and babysit with that."

She couldn't keep the tears back. She was so scared that she wouldn't get to see Art today, and she was afraid, too, that her mother might suspect what she was really going to do. She just knew her guilt showed her face, so she ran out the door and down to the trail to the river. She stopped close enough to see the driveway to the house. She just stood there not knowing what to do, then she saw her mother and Jimmy come out and get into the car. She was so relieved that she almost wanted to stop the car and apologize, but she dared not. Let well enough alone. It was only a short while before she saw the dark green convertible coming down the road. She felt her heart in her throat. She had thought about asking him into her house now that Mama and Jimmy were gone for a few hours, but then she remembered Carla and how frightened she was that her mother would come home all the time. Julia knew that wasn't where she wanted to give herself to Art.

CHAPTER VI

THE FEELING OF LOVE

As the car stopped, she didn't wait to be asked. She opened the door and hopped in. This time, not sitting so far away. He was more handsome than ever, with his dark eyes set off by a gold-colored knit shirt and that ever-present smile.

"Hi, little one." She noted a strangely soft tone to his voice like she had heard her mother use toward Jimmy.

"Look, I'm not your daughter, so please don't use that tone of voice that sounds like it."

"I didn't mean it to sound that way. I've thought of you all night, and no matter how I feel about you, you are little, you are young, and you are lovely. In my thoughts, you became my *little one* but not as a daughter, I assure you. If you don't like it, I'll change it."

"No, I do like it. I hope you'll always call me that. Even when I'm old and ugly." They both laughed at that. The thought of her being old and ugly didn't seem possible. After all, now, she was attractive and she knew it. She had red hair, fair complexion, blue eyes, and a large mouth that would turn very sensuous especially when she used the expression that made it so.

She didn't ask him where they were going, and he didn't mention anything that would remotely give her a hint. They just drove and talked. She found out that he was from Dallas, that he was a rancher and a cattle buyer for a market association, that he had been raised in the country until he ran away at the age of fifteen. He had worked at everything, from merchant seaman to ditch digger. "A helluva good one, though," as he had said. He asked questions about her but she would always turn back to his life. She was fascinated because she had never known anyone like him before. He was tough, plenty tough. "You had to be, in the Merchant Marine." He also loved animals, "especially the little ones because they look so helpless, like a baby waiting for its mother to pick it up." He had been equally at home in the Governor's House or at the hobo camp where he landed once when he didn't have a dime. He got the name of each hobo that was there, and later had helped most of them start something resembling a life.

When the car stopped, she noticed they were at a restaurant-motel. She had told him that she hadn't had breakfast, so he very nonchalantly went inside, leaving her in the car and wondering who was watching her. She looked down at the car seat the whole time he was in the restaurant. He handed her a sack that smelled of doughnuts and a key that said #19. He didn't say anything, just drove to the room and stopped in front. He got out and came around to open her door, took the key from her hand, and opened the motel door. She went inside as if she had done things like this all her life. He locked the door, took the sack and her purse, put them on the desk, then drew her toward him and kissed her so hard that she found herself gasping for breath. Then, just as if they were in an office, he took her by the arm, seated her at the desk, and took out the milk straw napkin, and told her to eat her breakfast while he watched TV. She didn't know whether to be angry that he seemed to take this all for granted or to be glad that he left her alone for a time to get used to the idea of being in a motel with a man she had just recently known.

The doughnuts made her feel better, but she felt rather uneasy. She didn't know what to do with herself after she had finished eating, so she went to the bathroom to was her hands. When she came out, he met her at the door and led her over to the chair. "I told you I'll never do anything you don't want me to do and you don't have to be afraid, remember?"

"Yes, but I've never been to a place like this. This way, that is. I don't know who might have seen me. I don't know what may happen. I just don't know."

"Little one, come here." As he patted the bed beside him, she got up and came over. "Just lay here a minute and rest. Get used to me a little. I've been listening to you and watching you, and I think I can pretty well tell what kind of girl you are, or rather, what kind of girl you've been raised to be. You've been taught that sex is not to be discussed. You've got a craving for love but you've never been loved. You think someone will see you and think you're cheap, don't you?"

"I guess, you're right. It bothers me what people think. I don't want anyone to think I'm cheap."

"Honey, you'll never be cheap. No matter what you do or where you go, you'll never be cheap. I knew the moment I looked into your eyes at the graduation ceremony that you weren't cheap. You have a lot of love buried in you, and you want to set it free. You want to set yourself free but something inside you keeps telling you it's wrong, or you'll be caught and punished, or maybe even hurt. I'll never knowingly hurt you. I won't ever let anyone else hurt you, either, if I can help it. I've been almost everywhere and done almost everything but I've never run across anyone that I could really love and know it's real, all real, until now. I do love you, little one." As he kissed her and leaned over her and stroked her breast and her thighs and her stomach, she knew at last the feeling of one who wants to give herself completely in love. "I love you, too, Art. I didn't really know the meaning of the word. I don't think until I saw you just two days ago, but I can't get you out of my mind. I almost got hysterical this morning when I thought I was going to stay home and watch my little brother. Oh Art, love me, really love me. Make me not afraid or ashamed. You know I've never done this before, but

I want you to make me hurt so much I can't stand it. Then love me, please!"

"Don't ever beg. Don't ever do that!" He almost shouted, and it wasn't really like him. She almost sat up, but he held her. "I'm sorry but it goes back a long way. I can't explain now, just believe me. You'll never have to beg for anything for as long as I live. I promise you that."

He got up and sat in the chair and leaned back and looked up at the satin ceiling a long time. Then he closed his eyes and she almost thought he was asleep, then he started to tell her about his wife. When he was through, he told her she could go out and get into the car if she wanted to and he'd take her back home and never see her again. She sat motionless for a while. So he had a wife and she only loved him when it would accomplish something for her. She used sex as a weapon, and no matter how he begged her sometimes, she wouldn't give in until she felt that she could get something out of it, like a new dress or a trip, or something that she really wanted. She didn't really know how she felt now. They sat in silence for a long time, then she got up and walked over to him.

"Art, I don't care that you have a wife. You don't love her. I know that. I may be a green kid just out of school, this may be my first time with a man but I know you don't love her, and you do love me, don't you?"

"You know I do, my little Julia, my little one. I'll love you till the day I go to hell, I guess."

She had never been kissed like how he kissed her. She didn't know when they undressed. What she knew was that beyond her wildest dream, she couldn't have dreamed a feeling of pure love's ecstasy like she felt at this moment. It couldn't ever end; never, for as long as she lived.

CHAPTER VII

THE NEW LIFE

"Why, in heaven's name, do you think you have to traipse off to Dallas to get a job and see things? We have plenty of jobs around here close enough to live at home. There's Rock Springs and Pleasantville, to name two of them. Eunice Canady's cousin has an insurance agency in Rock Springs, and she told me yesterday she was sure she could help you get on as a claims girl or something. You could make much more money if you'd stay home and work there. Then you wouldn't have to pay rent. Besides, if you go way up there, I don't know when we'll get to see you."

"I don't intend to stay here, that's all. I've baby-sat with Jimmy for you for ten years, Mother, and now you'll have to get someone else. I don't intend to stay here another night. I'm leaving on the 4:00 a.m. bus and I already have my ticket."

"Where did you get the money for that?"

"I've saved every penny I could for six months just to be able to afford that. I'll stay with Louise or some of the girls that I know who are already there. If I can't find one of them, I'll at a motel." She lied about the money. Art had given it to her.

"You wouldn't! A young, single girl staying at a motel all alone. What will people think?"

"Mother, there are so many people up there. No one will care one way or the other. I have to get busy and pack, I only have four hours before the bus."

She didn't tell her mother that she wouldn't be alone that night. She had talked to Art yesterday and told him when she would arrive, and he would be there to meet her and take her to a motel where they could be alone. It had been almost a month since he had been there with her those very short hours. He told her when he left that she would probably forget him and never see him again. She had been so lonely when he left that she could hardly stand it. She had spent hours down at the river just dreaming. She didn't even want Greg along. The last time he had asked her to go fishing with him, she had gotten irritated and told him that she didn't want to spend her life *messing around with young kids.*

Greg had looked at her that day, as if suddenly, a realization had come over him that would explain her actions lately. He stood there gazing at her so intently that she had found herself blushing.

"You've been doing something that's wrong, Julia. I wasn't sure until today what it was, but now I think I do."

"You don't have any idea at all. I just don't like spending so much time with you, that's all. What can it possibly gain me? You want to stay here in this place and work at that garage and that's all. Well, I don't intend to waste my life in this godforsaken place anymore. The only thing I've done is dream a little. And what more, I'm going to make those dreams come true, too. You'll see." She was in tears by the time she reached the safety of the shade by the river. She knew Greg was right. She knew it was wrong. After all, hadn't she had taught to her all her life by her mother, the minister, her Sunday school teachers, everyone. "Thou shalt not…."

Somehow, though, as she thought about Art, she couldn't make herself think anything was wrong with the way she felt about him. She wouldn't let herself think about his wife. After all, hadn't he told her how miserable she treated him? How could any woman treat him that way? He was so kind, gentle, so sensitive to her touch. "I'll go!" she said it out loud. "I'll go tomorrow. I'll call him now and tell him I'll be there tomorrow." She wanted to shout it. She was so happy with her decision. She walked back along the trail to the road, then turned toward town. She would call him collect at the office and tell him. That way, she wouldn't have to go home at all until she got her answer.

Now it was time to catch the bus, and she had a feeling in the pit of her stomach that almost made her nauseous. She didn't think it was fear of leaving home as much as anticipation for the unknown. As she was closing her suitcase, Jimmy came into the room. He walked over to the bed and looked down at the suitcase.

"Jule, I'm going to miss you." As he spoke, there were tears from the beginning to form. For the first time in his life, Julia actually felt a sort of love for him. There he stood, almost crying and telling her he would miss her. Did he mean he'd miss her looking after him, picking up after him, cleaning his room, helping him with his lessons, or would he really miss her? "I'll be back soon to see you. Besides, now you'll get to do anything you want and won't have to worry about me telling on you."

"I don't care about your telling on me. When I'm mean, you ought to tell. I just couldn't make myself do the right things until you'd tell on me and Mama would make me. Now, Who's going to tell on me so Mama will make me do right?"

"Well, I guess, maybe you'll just have to tell on yourself now. Maybe my going away is going to be good for you. I'll sort of miss you, too." He threw his hands around her waist and hugged her tightly, so tightly he almost broke her back, and then ran out of the room. She found herself crying a little, too. Why did it take so long for her to realize that she actually loved him? She would come back soon, if for no other reason, to see him and see if he had been benefited from her leaving.

"Greg's outside. I told him this morning you were going to take the eleven a.m. bus and he asked me if he could take you. I thought it'd give you time to say good-bye to him. I wish you'd stay here and maybe marry him. He has that nice job at the garage, and your Papa said Greg was going to be promoted to manager before long."

"You said I had been spending too much time with Greg, don't you remember?" She couldn't resist that bit of sarcasm as her last official act at home. Afterwards, she was sorry, for that was to be her last time to see her mother alive. But she couldn't have known that now. All she wanted now was to get on the bus and get to Art's arms. Nothing else mattered. Nothing.

"Here, let me have your bag. It looks pretty heavy." She noticed Greg wasn't looking her straight in the eye. "I appreciate your driving me to the bus. At least, I have Mama out of the way now and Jimmy, too. Do you know he cried when he told me bye? I guess he does like me, after all."

"Like you! You selfish little squirt. You're always so all fired up, ready to criticize if everything isn't going your way. You can't even see what's going on around you. That kid loves you so much he can't stand to see you leave. The only reason he does things to you is to get you to notice him. He knows you don't care about him and that's the only way he knows of telling you he loves you. If you weren't so damn selfish, you'd see that with your own eyes. And while I'm at it, you're pretty damn mean to your mother, too. You know she hasn't been feeling very good, and you could stay and help her with the housework a little while longer until she gets up on her feet. But, no! You have to go to Dallas so you can be on your *own* and do what *you* please. You may find you can miss us down here. They're not going to give a damn about you up there. You're not going to have people tell you 'Hi' when you walk down the street like they do here. They're not going to care. I hope you get so damn lonely you get sick and have to come back. Maybe that would knock some sense into you. You've got to see for yourself. You know how I feel about you but that doesn't matter, either. Well, I hope they're rough on you. I think it's about time you paid for some of the heartaches you've caused. Here's the bus stop. You can wait by yourself. Goodbye, Julia!"

She watched the car drive away, and strangely enough, she had a feeling of loneliness already. She thought if she could tell Greg, he would feel good already, knowing she felt lonely. Anyway, she wouldn't for long. She would be having dinner with Art tonight in a private place and he would make love to her and she would forget everything before tonight existed. She'd show them; all of them.

She had been on the bus about hours; she guessed by looking at the sunset. She must be getting close for they would arrive at 8:40. Just as it was getting dark, the bus turned a curve around a hill and there, stretched out before her, lay a sea of sparkling lights as if they were with millions of spotlights shining upon them. She had never seen such a sight. As far as she could see, there were lights and more lights. Some colored, some taller than others. Some in lines as if they were streetlights, then the skyline standing majestically in the center. She was awestruck with its beauty. She had never thought what it would look like. Even the blinking red lights atop the radio towers were beautiful. Then, suddenly, she felt sick. There was that strange feeling in the pit of her stomach again. What if Art wasn't there? What if she were alone in a strange town? She really had no idea of the whereabouts of her girlfriends. That had just been a cover-up for Mama. Where would she go? She stared at the panorama of lights and felt tears streaming down her face. She quickly wiped them away with the back of her hand and decided not to worry. After all, if he wasn't there, all she had to do was go to a hotel for the night and call his office the next day.

The bus was in the midst of the lights now—theater marquee lights and restaurant lights, storefronts that she had only seen in ads. They pulled into the bus station. It was as big as a whole block. There were so many people she suddenly panicked. How on earth would she see Art, or would he find her? It come to a stop, and the passengers got up and started toward the front of the bus. As she approached the front, she looked out the window and there he was. As she stepped from the bus, he flashed that warm smile and took her by the hand. She felt like everything was going to be alright forever. Art would take care of her, and there's no need to worry. They got her bags and he carried them to the convertible. They didn't say much until they were in the car. Then he leaned over and kissed her.

"Hi, little one."

"Oh, Art, I was so afraid that you wouldn't be there or that something would happen. I've never seen so many lights, so many people."

"Honey, you don't ever have to be afraid. I'll always take care of you as long as I live. I'm so glad to see you. You didn't forget me?"

"Silly, how could I forget you? I've thought of nothing else hardly since you left. Can we go somewhere quiet?"

As the car pulled out of the parking lot, she felt so good. She had a warm feeling. She knew she was Art's. She'd never be anyone's but his.

"Hey, wake up, little one."

She didn't know what time it was, and for a moment couldn't figure out where she was, either. Then she sat up and saw him sitting on the side of the bed with glass milk and the donut.

"Sorry to wake you up but I have to go to the office. I'll call you later. Why don't you eat and go back to sleep? You had a hard day yesterday."

"Where am I? I've forgotten what the name of this place is or where it is."

"You're in the Cabana Hotel. It's two blocks from my office. Instead of calling you later, I may just come over. Now go back to sleep when you finish. I love you."

As he kissed her, she felt the warm, passionate love that she had felt from him that first time he had loved her. She couldn't be happier, she decided. As he shut the door behind him, she sat eating her donut and thinking about the future. What would she do?

She couldn't just be here in the Cabana Hotel all the time. She wanted a job close to Art, maybe even in his office.

The more she thought about it, the more it seemed terrifying. She could see him all day when he was in the office, then be with him at night, too. He only went home when he had to, anyway. Now, maybe he wouldn't go home at all. As she thought about the days ahead, she wondered what would be happening back home. How would her mother be without her? And then there was Jimmy. He had seemed so sad at her leaving. She decided they would be better off without her, though. Maybe Papa and Mama would even be lonely enough for her that they would love one another again. They must have loved each other at one time. After all, Mama had gotten pregnant twice, hadn't she? She thought about her own beautiful memory of Art making love to her, and then she tried to put Mama and Papa into that beautiful passionate surrounding. For the life of her, she couldn't imagine them feeling passion or love like she had. They must have felt something, or they wouldn't have gotten married. Maybe, as Art told her, she was unusual. He had said that he had never heard anyone talk about wives who really enjoyed being loved. With most men, their sexual relationship with their wife was a Saturday night affair, and only then if their wife felt like it.

As she sat there in bed thinking about her life, the telephone rang. It startled her. She hadn't thought about having to answer the phone.

"Hello," she answered in a hushed voice.

"Hi, little one. I just wanted to make sure you hadn't run out on me."

"Oh, Art, how could you think anything of the kind? You know I love you so much. I was just sitting here in bed thinking about how I love you. Art, am I really different from most women?"

"Yes. But I can't go into details over the phone right now, understand?"

"I think I do. Are you coming over after a while?" As she thought of him coming in that door, she found herself longing for him to hold her again.

"I'll be over about twelve. I'll bring us some hamburgers and French fries so we can eat lunch together. Would you like that?"

"Oh yes. I have something I want to ask you when you get here."

"The answer is no. I don't have that much time."

"Oh, Art, silly. Not that. I have something serious I want to tell you. See you at twelve." As she listened for his good-bye and hung the phone on the receiver, she got dressed in a beautiful pink sun suit. Pink looked good with her color hair. She had seen some redheads who couldn't wear pink at all because theirs wasn't the right color. But pink was one of her best colors.

She stood in front of the mirror looking at herself, gesturing at her reflection as if she were talking to someone. She knew how best to use her eyes and her hands to achieve the best effect. She had watched a lot of movies where the women would gesture or flirt with their eyes. She would come home and spend hours before the mirror in her room imitating them. She knew she was sexy and very attractive. But, right now, all she wanted to do was convince Art to help her get a job in his office. If she had to use some of her feminine tricks to do it, she would. She had rehearsed what she would say at least fifty times when she heard his key in the door. As she went to meet him, she thought how much of that smile of his always melted her. She wondered if he knew the effect it had on her. Some time she would tell him but not now.

She let him take off his coat and she set the hamburgers and French fries on the coffee table, fixed two glasses of ice water, then sat down. Even though she had rehearsed what she would say over and over, now that she was looking at him, she completely forgot how to begin.

"What's the matter, little one? You're not unhappy about anything, are you?"

"Well, kind of, I guess." She thought now was the perfect time to spring her idea. "Art, I love being with you and I know today is the first day here, but I can't sit in a room all day long doing nothing. I have to get a job."

"I've been thinking about that this morning, too. I've made arrangements to be out of the office tomorrow, and I thought we might look around for an apartment for you and maybe find a job for you, too. What would you really like to do? Have you ever thought about it?"

"Yes, I want to work in your office." She said it so fast and furious that he looked to see if she was alright. Her heart was pounding so hard, just like the day she first saw him. "Oh please, please, Art. I've thought it out, and it is the most sensible thing to do. If I were at another office and you had to call me, you'd have to ask for me by my name. and if I called for you, I'd have to leave my name if you weren't here and that wouldn't be wise. If I work in your office, all you would have to do is come by my desk or something. Oh please."

She was out of breath when she got through and she looked so appealingly at him, with all the appeal that she could muster, as excited as she was. Art laughed, then thought better of it and apologized because he could see it embarrassed her. She thought he laughed at her because she wanted to work with him.

"I'm sorry honey. I didn't laugh because I think the idea is funny. It's just that you were rattling on so fast that I couldn't believe you didn't breathe the whole time. You must have been doing a lot of thinking about this since I left you this morning. You might have a point, though. It might be the best thing after all for you to be there in the office. I tell you what. I'll talk to the personnel office when I go back this afternoon. I'll tell them that my nephew talked me into helping you find a job, and that I'd like you to be in my office so I can help you. It might just work, too, because there is a clerk that is leaving next week. We'll see."

CHAPTER VIII

The Red Pajamas

After Art had left, Julia decided this was a chance to get out on her own and see the big city. She had five hours before he would get back, so he took her key, looked in the mirror to be sure her lipstick wouldn't be smeared, and left. This was the first time she had seen the big city in the daylight. It wasn't as romantic looking as it had been at night with all the lights. She looked upward at the tops of the buildings, some gray with time, some shiny and new. As she walked up Main Street, she noticed one building with mirrors all over it. They were colored mirrors that gave her appearance an eerie look. *Like a zombie,* she thought. It was still the lunch hour and all the streets were flooded with workers going to and from lunch, some in suits, some in shirtsleeves, some looked happy, some bored. She wondered how she would look when she went to lunch after she started to work. She made herself a promise that she wouldn't look as dull and bored as some of the people she saw. She went into one of the big department stores and went up the escalator. She just looked at some of the things. She saw the most adorable red shortie pajama set and she wondered if she dared get it. She looked at the price tag—$14.95—new, and she had $20.00 left. She knew Art would get her a job, and he would get her an apartment, too. This once, she thought, she'd do something that she had always wanted to do. She had seen sets like these in magazines, and she always wanted to see what she would look like in one. She'd take it!

As she walked up the street, her pajamas in a box clutched tightly under her arm, she wondered what Mama and Jimmy were doing. She wondered if Papa were angry at her for leaving. He had been on a trip when she left. He went on trips often lately. She had asked him one time where he went and what he did, and he just said it was business and that was the end of the conversation. She had heard Papa and Mama arguing one night about a trip. She couldn't hear really well through the wall, but it had something to do with a motel bill somewhere that Papa's wasn't supposed to be. Papa wouldn't argue. He just stomped out the door, and she heard the car squeal as he left. When Papa did that, it was quite evident he was angry. She never mentioned hearing to Mama, and neither did Mama mention where Papa went anymore. When she would ask where Papa was. Mama would say "He went away on business and he'll be back when he finishes," and that was it.

She went back to the motel about 5:00 p.m. She showered and hurriedly tried her red pajamas to see if they fit. She looked into the mirror and smiled at herself. She was sexy and she knew it. She knew Art would approve. She changed into some shorts and was resting Art got back. She didn't get up; just looked at him. It was amazing to her how just looking at him made her hurt with passion. He came over to the bed and leaned down, looking at her with those dark, piercing eyes, the reached under her with his arms and raise her to him.

"I don't know whether it's good or bad, but I love you more than life itself. I could hardly wait to get here just now. All day, your red hair and blue eyes have been in my thoughts. And your arms around me, kissing me." He could talk no longer. His throat felt dry. His mouth on hers, that's all he wanted. It was as if they were one, of one accord and meaning—one fleshy, one desire. Julia had never known how beautiful love would be, and this was love at its fullest. She never wanted it to end. Never.

Afterward, she tried on the pajamas for him and they both laughed. They had been bought especially for him, and she had just forgotten all about them. After that, the red pajamas would be their joke between themselves. They never really ever got worn more than five minutes. "I don't need them. All I need is you," Art would say each time as he would carefully take them off her, loving her all the time. He knew they were a symbol to her. A symbol of her love for him.

CHAPTER IX

THE NEW JOB

As she entered the building with him, she noticed that was more formal with her. It bothered her until she realized this would have to be his manner with her all the time in the office. She decided that to see him during the day and work with him, she could be formal. At least, that long.

"Julia Watson, meet Ray Wheaton. Ray, this is the girl I told you about yesterday."

"Sit down, Julia. Art tells me you're up from a small town trying to find a job. Tell me, what can you do? I mean, type, shorthand, Dictaphone?"

"I took all those in business administration in high school. I like any type of office work, and I'm a good typist."

"Good. I'll take you down to the personnel office and you can fill out the papers down there, and then someone will bring you back up, Art. I think you've got a good girl here."

As they went down the elevator to the first-floor personnel office, Mr. Wheaton asked her how long she had known Art and she told the story they had agreed upon. She went to school with his nephew, and James had asked Art to help her get a job. The application papers were easy and the whole thing took about thirty minutes, then one of the girls from personnel took her back up to the office where she had met Mr. Wheaton. As they were going up in the elevator, the girl gave her a look of envy and told her how lucky she was to be working with Mr. Runyon, that he was so good looking and nice. Julia felt a twinge of pride knowing she was Mr. Runyon's favorite girl. She wished she could tell anyone that she was, but she knew this would always be impossible.

When Julia got back to Mr. Wheaton's office, he asked her to sit down. He asked her some things about what she had done. She admitted she had never done any of the things in a real office but she was willing to learn anything she had to know, plus anything else she could learn about any other job. She was really eager to learn anything she could about Art's office. Mr. Wheaton took her out to the desk where a girl was busily putting pages in a binder.

"Marita, this is Julia. She will be taking over your desk when you leave next week. Show her everything you can about the job, will you?" Turning to Julia, he added, "I'm sure you won't know everything at once, so please feel free to ask any of us and we'll try to help you. We're one big happy family here, and we try to keep it that way."

"I saw Mr. Runyon bring you into the office this morning. Have you known him long?" Marita had a look of *sees all, knows all* about her, so Julia thought if she put the story out by Marita, it would soon be all over the office and she wouldn't have to answer that question again.

"I met him at my graduation exercise. I went to school with his nephew and Jimmy asked Mr. Runyon if he could help me get job when I got moved up here, then I got in day before yesterday. I called Mr. Runyon and he told me you were leaving. I hope I'm not too dumb and can learn a lot about this job before you leave."

"Oh, you will. It's not that hard, really. First, I'll show you the things in the office that you'll need to know, the we'll go around and meet everyone." Julia noticed that Marita pointedly told each person as she introduced Julia to them that "Mr. Runyon's nephew is a friend of Julia's, and he asked his uncle if he would help her get a job up here." *It worked,* Julia thought. Now she would be through with the questions. At least, in this office.

As she typed and did odd things that Marita could show her right away, he would be looking at her. She thought of how it would be—trying not to catch each other's eyes, trying not to show how much she loved him with just a look. She would have to be careful, she decided. Very careful. Just before lunch, Art walked over to the to the desk. "Marita, do you think she is hopeless or can she be taught?" He was winking at her and smiling so she would know he was teasing.

"She's going to be fine, Mr. Runyon. She catches on quickly to things. She'll probably be running desk by tomorrow and you will be wanting to get rid of me before next week."

"Oh now, Marita, you know things just won't be the same around here without you. We will all miss you. If Julia is half as good as you, we won't complain." Marita blushed a little and bent down to the desk drawer. Art caught Julia long to catch on to the job. She could have done it by herself after the second day but she let Marita show her things time after time to make Marita feel good that this new girl wasn't such a whiz kid. Julia knew it is nice to be missed or to feel like you're missed. She missed Mama and Jimmy, and of all things, she actually missed Greg. Why on earth, she had no idea. But she found herself sitting at the desk one day thinking about him and the day he kicked him and he fell into the river. She must have been smiling herself because one of the girls walked by and said, "What's so funny?"

"Oh, nothing." Julie decided she'd have to be careful what she thought about, as well as what she did and said. But she liked it, anyway. She got to work with Art some. Some of the price sheets that he needed to have for his buying trips were her job to fix, so she worked closely with him at times. Sometimes if they were working closely and no one was around, Art would hold her hand, or pat her thigh and whisper under his breath, "Love you," and she would invariably look up to see if anyone was looking.

CHAPTER X

LEARNING TO FACE LOSS

The fourth week she was at work, she answered the phone as usual and was startled that the voice was Greg's. "Jule, I had to come up to a seminar at the technical college and I'll be here tonight. I'd like to take you to dinner."

She was going to tell him that she couldn't, then she remembered that Art would fly out in the afternoon for a two-day buying trip. "I'd love to, Greg. Where are you staying?"

"At the Hilton. Do you want me to pick you up at work or your apartment?"

"I'll meet you at the Hilton. About six, okay?" She certainly didn't want Greg to walk in the apartment and see all of Art's clothes in the closet and his things all over the place.

"Okay, see you at six, and Jule…."

"Yes, Greg."

"It's wonderful to hear your voice again. See you."

As she walked into the lobby of the Hilton, she saw Greg. To her surprise, she was excited at the sight of this tall, lean boy who was only a few months older than she was. He saw her come in and jumped up, rushed over, and hugged and kissed her. She was so glad to see him she didn't care who saw them at that moment.

"Gee, you look beautiful. It seems like a year since I've seen you."

"It's so good to see you, too, Greg. How is everybody? You know, Mama and Jimmy?"

She noticed a shadow come over his face, then he looked at his watch and said, "Why don't we go somewhere before they get crowded? I'd love a big, thick steak. Where shall we go?"

"Cattlemen's is the best, I think. We'll have to take a taxi. I don't feel like the walk." She kept looking at Greg all the way in the taxi, and tried to ask about Mama and Jimmy and he put it off saying he'd tell her all about it when they got to the restaurant where he wouldn't have to stop so much. She had forebodings of something wrong, maybe terribly wrong. She waited patiently until they were seated and had ordered, then she looked him straight in the eye and asked, "Greg, what's the matter? Something's the matter with Mama and Jimmy, isn't there? That's really the reason you're here, isn't it?" She was almost panicky and she started to cry.

"Jule, calm down. It's not what you think. There is something wrong, and you might as well know now. Your mother and father are getting a divorce."

Julia sat there looking blankly at Greg. He reassured her it was true and told her some of the details as Mama had told him to, but she couldn't believe it. She knew Mama and Papa had never been close. She knew she had wondered if they were ever close to one another, but Papa had always come home after his trips. He paid the bills and gave Mama money for shopping, and gave Jimmy some money every now and then for something. He had been home enough that this just didn't seem possible. She remembered the motel bill—Mama and Papa—had argued about. After that, Mama wouldn't say anything about where he was or what he was doing, just *business*. All sorts of things were going on in her mind. She suddenly came back to reality and realized Greg was talking.

"The doctor says it may not be serious but she must have absolute rest. No work at all. Just bed rest."

"What did you say?"

"Jule, weren't you listening? Your mother had a heart attack when the divorce papers arrived. She is in the hospital now, but the doctor says it appears to be a light one. I told him that I would drive up and get you. I had just gotten to the edge of town when I called you. I knew I couldn't drive right back, so I thought it best to get a night's sleep before we go back early in the morning. I couldn't just pick you up at the office and tell you all this. I want you to eat something and I'll take you home and we'll leave at daybreak in the morning. We'll be home by noon. The doctor said she would need you more when she comes home from the hospital than now because she must have complete bed rest, and you're the only one that can give her that"

Finally, it came over to what was happening and what Greg was saying. She would have to leave Dallas, her job, and Art, and go home to take care of her mother. He didn't know what he was asking her, or rather telling her. She couldn't leave. But she would go home and see her mother and give Papa a piece of her mind, then get someone to stay with her. Art would help her. Art! Where was he going to be tonight?

"Greg, I want to make a phone call. Excuse me, and I'll be right back. I have to inform someone at the office." She dug through her purse and she found the schedule Art had given her of his trip. Houston. That was where he was tonight. She placed a collect call to him at his hotel. After endless questions and rings, he finally answered.

"Oh, Art. Something terrible has happened." She began to cry and couldn't talk.

"Come on, little one. Calm down a little and tell me. Are you alright?"

"Yes, I'm alright. But Mama… Mama had a heart attack." She didn't know exactly what he said because she was crying so hard, but she knew he had to go on down and he would tell the office. He would be down as soon as he got back from his trip if she wanted him to. She managed to say yes and hung up.

They ate some, not much. She could hardly get a bite down. When Greg wanted to drive her to her apartment, she persuaded him to let her take a cab so he could get more rest. She got home, packed, and tried to sleep, but it was almost impossible.

Finally, at 4:00 a.m., she got dressed and called Greg's room.

"Hello, Jule."

"How did you know it was me?"

"Because I knew you wouldn't sleep and you'd be up early and ready to go, so I left a 3:00 a.m. call. I'm ready and I'll pick you up in fifteen minutes."

"I'll be out front."

As they drove back, she remembered the bus ride she had only taken four weeks ago. Was it only four weeks? All the things that had happened? Everything was enmeshed with Art. Her job, her apartment, her trip. How she wished he was here now. But Greg was so sweet. She sat looking at him and remembering the first ride she had taken with Art. They're so different, how in the world could she like both of them? She didn't love Greg. That was the difference.

"Greg, it was so sweet of you to come up after me like this. I hope it didn't hurt your job."

"It didn't. I told Mr. Greenfield what happened and he told me to go ahead. He knows I like you a lot."

"How could he possibly know that? I've never even met him."

"Simple. I told him." He had such a pleased look on his face, she shouldn't be angry with him. After all, he had driven to Dallas to get her. She didn't know what she would have done if he hadn't.

They didn't talk much after that. She thought about Papa. She had never been extra fond of Papa, but he was her Papa. Now, she hated him. He was the cause of all this. There had to be another woman, and Papa was divorcing Mama to marry her. There was always another woman. Hadn't she heard Mama and Mrs. Middleton discuss someone last year who was getting a divorce because there was another woman? Funny she should think of that now because she realized she was the *other woman* in Art's life. For the first time, she would like to see Art's wife. She'd like to know what she looked like and what kind of person she was. She didn't know how but she would do it when she got back to Dallas.

When they arrived at the house, there were three cars parked in front. One was Papa's, one was Mrs. Middleton's, and she thought the other one was Reverend Ashley's. Since Mama was in the hospital, Mrs. Middleton was probably helping with the house and Jimmy. When they got out of the car, Greg put his arm around her and they walked up the path Mrs. Middleton came out onto the porch to meet them. She had been crying. Julia knew because her mascara was running. She hugged Julia and tried to say something but started crying again. Panic took hold of Julia. She knew this was something more than a light heart attack.

"Mrs. Middleton, how is Mama?" She started crying, too. She knew intuitively Mama was in severe condition. Reverend Ashley came out to take her by the hand. He led her into the house and told her to sit down. She heard Jimmy crying in the back bedroom. As she looked at him, her eyes welling over with tears, she was shaking her head sideways. "No, no. Tell me she isn't"

"She has gone to join the angels, Julia. She went in her sleep. There was no pain."

Julia didn't hear any of what she said. She was sobbing so hard she could hardly breathe. Not Mama. Greg sat beside her, holding her as she cried.

"If we had only come straight back, we could have been here."

"No, it wouldn't have done any good. She died at six last evening. We knew you would have just gotten there, and we knew if we called you'd have come straight back and you had to have some rest. Besides, Jimmy needs his sister now more than ever and we wanted to be sure you got here safely."

"Jimmy." She rushed into the back bedroom where he was lying face down on the bed and picked him up. They held on tight to each other, sobbing. It was a long time before they could do anything.

"Oh, Jule. I'm so glad you're here. Mama's gone. Papa's run off with another woman. He doesn't want me. You're all I got. Oh please, don't leave, Jule. Promise. Please."

"Yes, I promise, Jimmy. We'll be together. Mama would've wanted it that way. Now don't cry. Let's wash our faces and get something to drink." She smoothed his hair and fixed his clothes. She realized now that he was her responsibility. Of course, Papa might cause trouble but he wasn't going to get Jimmy. She realized the antidote to grief was hate because she began to hate Papa with every fiber of her being. She calmly smoothed her hair, splashed some water on her eyes, powdered her nose, and came back into the living room. As she entered, she looked.

"Papa, you can go ahead and do whatever it was you were going to do before Mama died. I will take care of Jimmy." She wondered if Papa would give her any trouble. He looked at her, then at Jimmy holding onto her so tightly, then back at her. He just sighed and walked out of the house, got into the car, and drove off. He didn't say a word to anyone. No, Papa wouldn't give her any trouble over Jimmy. He didn't want to be bothered with anything, not even his children. She decided at the moment she didn't care if she ever saw him again. Now she could understand Mama better, knowing what she must have suffered through while Julia was growing up. As she was thinking about where Papa was going to with another woman somewhere, suddenly it flashed before her mind. She had never even asked Art if he had children. Why hadn't she asked? She really had never even thought about it until now. Now that Papa was leaving his children for someone she didn't even know. How could she feel this way about Papa when she was that woman Art left for his wife and possibly children for? She just stood hugging Jimmy, as the tears began to etch their path down her cheek. Everything would be alright. She knew it.

Somehow, she managed to live through the next day with Mrs. Middleton's and Greg's help. She arranged for her mother's funeral. She didn't know how it would be paid for but Mr. Simmons had known Mama and Papa both and he said he would get in touch with Papa. He put a fatherly arm around Julia as she left and patted her shoulder. "Have faith, Julia. I'm sure the Lord knew best. You wouldn't have wanted her to be an invalid and that is what might have happened. She wouldn't have wanted it that way. Everything will work out for the best, you'll see. Don't worry about anything. I'll contact your father." He gave her a reassuring hug as he helped her into Greg's car.

They didn't say a word on the way home. Her thoughts were on the future. What would she do about Jimmy? Where would she live? What about Art? Oh Art. If she could only see him now. She was still in deep thought when they rounded the hill overlooking the river and their house, and there in front of the house was Art's green convertible. She suddenly got panic-stricken. What would she tell Greg? She just wanted to be alone with Art for a while. Jimmy was at Mrs. Middleton's. As they got out, Art came out of the house with Reverend Ashley, shook his hand, and came toward Julia. He put his arm around her in a fatherly way, and told Greg he came down from the office to see if they could do anything to assist Julia. He shook Greg's hand and asked Julia if she would like to take a ride, maybe she would feel better if she got away from these familiar surroundings. She couldn't talk. She just shook her head, and Art helped her into the car.

"We'll be back in a little while. I just think she should get away from this house for a little while. Her brother will be taken care of for a little while, won't he?" Greg and Reverend Ashley both agreed that Jimmy was alright, and told Julia to go. Maybe she'd feel better to get her mind off her grief for a while.

They drove up the river road where they had gone that first day and parked at the picnic area overlooking the river. Julia just at close to him all the way and didn't say anything. Just his closeness seemed to calm and reassure her that it would be alright; everything would work out. She didn't even care what Greg or Reverend Ashley or anyone else thought. She just knew she needed Art now more than ever before. Art held her in his arms and she began to cry. He just stroked her hair and held her for a long time, then he kissed her. It seemed she hadn't ever cried like that before. She didn't know whether it was grief or happiness. She didn't know how long it was before she calmed enough to talk.

"Thank you. I didn't know how much I needed you and depended on you." She took his handkerchief and dried her eyes and took her compact and powdered her nose. "My goodness I look like a witch, don't I?" She managed half a laugh.

"Of course, you don't. Now if you're calm enough to talk, tell me. Anything and everything you want to. You know I love you and I'll do anything I can to help you. Now tell me." He leaned back in the seat and looked at the sky, waiting for her to talk. She finally told him everything—about the divorce, and Greg coming after her, about Papa and the other woman. Then suddenly, she remembered something.

"Art, I want to know. Do you have any other children?" She noticed a shadow come over his usual calm, pleasant face. He looked straight ahead for a while, then looked at her with a questioning glance, then sighed. She saw it was difficult to answer. "If you don't want to tell me, it's alright."

"I'll tell you, but first, I want to know why you asked at this particular time."

She told him about Papa and the other woman, and how she had begun to realize she was the other woman and how she felt about Papa leaving her and Jimmy for someone else. She blurted it all out, all her feelings of guilt that had become so vivid these last two days.

Art sat there thinking. "My poor little one. You've been feeling cheap again, haven't you?" He kissed her lightly on the forehead and held her hand. He knew by her eyes that she had been feeling guilty and cheap and no telling what else.

"Listen to me. I told you that first day I loved you. That you should never feel cheap. Remember? What I feel for you comes along once in a lifetime. I never felt that way about my wife or anyone else. I felt something for my wife when I met and married her, but not what I feel for you. You know I don't lie. That's the truth. Now since your father has left you and Jimmy and you know he has another woman, you feel dirty because you put yourself in that woman's place. There's a lot of difference. To answer your question, no, I do not have any children. I had a son. He died when he was ten years old. He had leukemia.

I think when he died, my wife and I realized that we didn't love one another. We never really did, I don't think. It was just that when the baby came along, we had a life in him and that's as far as it went. Now ours is just a marriage of convenience. She has her life and I have mine. Does all this shock or disturb you?" He was watching her eyes intently to see if he could tell any look of disdain or anger or anything.

"No, it doesn't shock or disturb me. I knew you didn't love your wife or you couldn't love me like you do. I know you love me." She leaned over and kissed him, and even now with her grief and turmoil, when she kissed him she felt so much passionate love for him that she hurt. "You're right. I did put myself in that other woman's category, though. I've done a lot of thinking since night before last and I've had to make a lot of decisions and some I have yet to make. One thing I know, Jimmy will live with me wherever I live. I don't know how or where or what's going to happen, but Papa will not have Jimmy." As she said this, he noted the cold glassy stare of hatred that came over her face. He had never seen her like this.

"Honey, there are a lot of things to do, but as far as I can, I'll help you. We'll face the future one day at a time. I can stay a couple of days to help you now, then we'll see after that. Now tell me, Greg is somebody special, isn't he?" He watched her face intently, trying to find about this boy who had driven 350 miles just to tell her the bad news and drive her home. He knew Greg thought she was something special.

He could tell the minute he saw Greg help her out of the car. Now he waited to hear Julia's answer.

"I've known him all my life. We've gone to school together, fished together, been to the movies together. He even asked me to marry him when I was fifteen. I love him like a brother. That's all. I don't know what I would have done without him though.

"You may love him like a brother, but that's not the way he loves you. I watched him help you out of the car and he put his arm around you and looked at you. You might as well face facts, little one. He's in love with you."

"Well, you may be right, but it's only his feelings. Not mine. You're the only one I've ever loved or ever intended to love. Take me somewhere and help me."

He decided it would help both of them to get off by themselves and love one another, to have her in his arms. He could have help her get rid of some torn up emotions that way. They drove to the same motel where he had first taken her. When they were in the room, they quickly undressed and we're in each other's arms before they knew it.

"I'm sorry I don't have my red pajamas with me."

"Those really don't anything for me. Those are for you. All I need is you."

The next day, the day of her mother's funeral, Julia got up early. She took a walk down to the river where she had gone so many times to think and dream. She was there when Art drove up. Mrs. Middleton told him where she was, and he started to walk down the trail. When he saw her, she was standing on the bank, staring out over the river. He wanted to watch her for a while. This little eighteen-year-old girl that he loved so much. She was so small. She had on a pink dress and her red hair was blooming in the breeze that was coming across the river. *She was a study in beauty and grace,* he thought as he watched her. Then she turned and started toward him before she knew he was there. She smiled as he came toward her.

"So this is where you used to dream about things. This is where you were going when I saw you that second time. It's really beautiful here. I don't blame you for coming here. I would be wonderful to sit here and think, and just to let the world go by." He sat down on a fallen tree and pulled her down beside him. "Honey, this is going to be a hard day for you. Do you want me to stay with you?"

"Oh yes. Please, stay with me all the time. I'll have Jimmy, and I need you to help steady me. Please, don't leave me." She was almost pleading.

"Alright, calm down. I just didn't know how it would look. You know, someone from your office being with you instead of Greg or Mrs. Middleton or someone."

"I don't care how it looks. I just know I need you with me every minute, Please."

"Alright, I will. Now don't worry. I'll try to help you with Jimmy, too. Afterwards, we'll talk about the future. Right now, let's go to the house. You have to get dressed. We have to be there at 11:00 a.m., and it's eight now." He took her by the arm and walked her back to the house. He knew she was dreading the service. That was only natural. He wondered if her father would be there, and if he was, what Julia would do. Anyway, he would stand by her all the time like he had promised. They left for the church shortly before eleven, just time enough to get seated. It was hard enough without having time to sit there and think too much. He had her beside him and Jimmy beside her. When the service started, he noticed her father come in and sit down in the row behind them. He didn't know whether Julia noticed or not. She had her eyes closed most of the time. After the service, Julia stopped and stared at her father—a blank stare. Jimmy saw him and held onto Julia even tighter. Art decided the best thing to do was to get them out of the church and into the car. He was relieved that her father didn't attend graveside service.

He helped Julia and Jimmy into his car, and got in. He looked at the two of them, holding on tight to each other and sobbing. He wanted to hold both of them but he couldn't. He had noticed the questioning looks he had gotten during the funeral and later in the cemetery. After all, people from the office usually didn't take such good care of their coworkers, especially one as new as Julia.

He knew now that Julia would have to bring Jimmy back to Dallas with her. That is, if her father gave his consent. Right now, his only thought was to get them out away somewhere to get their minds off their troubles.

"Say, anybody hungry but me?" He had started toward the restaurant motel. The one he and Julia had gone to.

"I guess, I am a little," Jimmy managed to say. He had been looking to Art to a lot without saying much. Julia told him Mr. Runyon was her boss, and that he had business in the area and came by to help.

"I guess, maybe I should eat something. And I know Jimmy should, too. Neither one of us had much appetite at breakfast, did we Jim?" She gave him a loving pat on the shoulder. Funny, but now that Mama was gone, she found she really loved Jimmy an awfully lot. She decided a lot of her dislike of him must have been jealousy. He got all the attention, she thought. But now that she had been away, Julie had thought it all out, "he was the youngest, the most trouble, and the one who needed more care. He should have gotten more attention than she got. It was one of the rules of growing up—you become independent. Strange she hadn't thought about that before.

They drove up to the restaurant side and parked, Jimmy said, "Oh boy, I haven't been here before." Art looked at Julia and smiled.

After they had ordered, Art asked Jimmy if he would like to go to the back window and look out at the river. Jimmy was delighted. He hadn't ever seen it from this high, and there was a barge coming down. While he was at the back, Art took Julia's hand.

"Honey, we have to talk about something. You can't stay here, you know that, don't you?" She shook her head. She knew, too. She had seen the glances. Jimmy must never know about them.

"What then?"

"Do you think your father will let Jimmy come to Dallas with you?"

"I've been thinking about that. Art, I don't want Jimmy to live with him and that woman. Besides, I love him and want him with me but we can't stay here. Even if I quit my job and moved into the house, how could I support us? Papa would pay some, I'm sure. But I don't know how much. You saw him at the church today."

"Yes, Art had seen him. A whipped, beaten man. Ashamed was more the word. He knew that everyone knew. Honey, where is your father now, do you know?"

"No. at that woman's house, I guess. But I don't know who she is. Mrs. Middleton might know. She was Mama's best friend. But knowing how close-mouthed Mama was, she might not have even told Mrs. Middleton.

"When we leave here, let's go to Mrs. Middleton's and find out. Don't tell Jimmy, though. If Mrs. Middleton knows where he is, we'll leave Jimmy with her and go see him."

"Now?" She felt her heart pounding so hard she thought it would jump out of her. She didn't know whether she could face Papa or not. After all, she had left home while he was on one of his *business trips* and she hadn't said a word to him since she got back.

"I'll go with you. I can tell him that you have a nice apartment in a nice part of town, and that you have a good job in my office. I could even tell him that my wife and I will help with Jimmy. He will never know. It's a chance, little one. If he doesn't agree, it will mean court action. After all, you've just turned eighteen yourself and no judge would give you custody of a ten-year-old. Let's face it, honey, we have to get his permission."

She knew he was right. But to face Papa! She found that she wasn't very hungry when their food was served. She couldn't remember the last time she had been hungry. She rehearsed what she would say to Papa. Nothing would be right, she knew that. But she had to try to keep calm. At least, until he gave Jimmy the right to go. She wanted it in writing, too, so he couldn't think about it and decide in a month or at his convenience to come after him. Art would know what to do.

It turned out, Mrs. Middleton did know who the woman was. As a matter of fact, Julia found out that everyone in town except her. Julia didn't know her in person. She had just heard the name in passing. They left Jimmy there and told him they would be back shortly, then they drove across town to where Lila lived. Mrs. Middleton told her Lila was a divorcee who has a little girl, six years old. She worked at the insurance office where Papa had been seeing her before she was divorced, and that was probably why her husband sued her for divorce.

The house was small, needing repairs in places, and a coat of paint. She found herself visualizing Papa painting the house and moving the lawn and repairing the roof. Things that he would never take care of on their house. Mama always had to call someone to get things done. Again, she put herself in Lila's place. She had been getting so much help and attention from Art. She was getting what his wife couldn't get this time. The past four weeks, she had been with him almost every day. Four weeks. Had it only been four weeks? It seemed impossible that so much had happened in less than a month. All at once, her wonderful life—her job, her apartment, her life together with Art—was threatened. She knew that if Jimmy stay with her, there would be no more nights alone with Art. At least, not in the apartment. Art was holding the door for her to get out of the car. She suddenly got weak. She hadn't counted on an open confrontation with Papa and his mistress.

"I can't do it. I can't go up on that porch and ask for Papa. I won't go in that house, either. If Papa hadn't been here, none of these things would have happened. Mama would still be alive and I would still be in my apartment with you," She stepped back against the car, leaning on it for support. "I just can't."

"Okay, honey, take it easy. I'll ask Mr. Watson to come out here and talk to you." He walked up to the porch and knocked on the door. Julia saw the door open and noticed a short, rather large woman with bleached hair look out toward her. Julia felt herself shrinking back inside the car. She didn't want to look at that woman in the face. Inside, she knew it was because she put up herself in that woman's place. As she was feeling remorse, guilt, maybe even shame, she saw Papa coming toward her. All at once, instead of feeling guilt or even grief, she knew nothing but anger at his sight. She saw Art looking at her hard, trying to let her know to calm down. With all the courage she had, she swallowed and said, "Hello, Papa."

"Who is this man, Jule?" He turned an accusing eye toward Art, then back at her.

Suddenly, she got the picture. To try to throw the suspicion away from him, he would accuse her of no telling what. She felt panic for a moment, then she looked at Art with a surprised look.

"Oh, I thought you knew Mr. Runyon. He's James Little's uncle. I work for him in Dallas." She didn't know whether it worked with Papa or not. He still looked at Art as if he hated everything about him. She wouldn't let this drag on any longer than necessary.

"Papa, Mr. Runyon has to go down to Houston tomorrow on business, and he has said he would be glad to stop back by on his way back to Dallas and take Jimmy and I back. You know you don't really want to have Jimmy to look after now that you have a new family, I mean." She gave it everything she had. She thought if she was nonchalant, not seeming to care one way or another, he might come nearer to letting Jimmy go. "I think I can work it out fine at my apartment if you'd like Jimmy to come home with me. I have a two-bedroom apartment in a nice neighborhood. The school is two blocks away. Mrs. Runyon sent word that she would help me out when I had to work overtime, or if Jimmy were sick or something. I suppose it would work alright. What do you think?" She looked at Art and he had a look of surprise, even almost a smile on his face. She wanted him to say something, so she gave him a look of helplessness. He took the hint.

"Mr. Watson, my wife and I are very fond of Julia and we would like very much enjoy helping with Jimmy. Our son died when he was ten, and it would be grand to have a boy around again. Of course, I know how it is with a son and I know you would like to keep him close and I don't want to sway your decision one way or the other. I know, too, how hard would it be for you, trying to work and having to have a housekeeper or someone to depend on. Jimmy seems so close to Julia, it would be a shame for them not to be together, don't you think?"

They both waited while Mr. Watson thought a moment. Julia was really proud of herself for not mentioning Lila. She had deliberately evaded saying anything about Mama, or the divorce, or anything, just Jimmy. She almost crossed her fingers behind her back while she waited for him to say something. Papa looked toward the house, then back to Julia. He seemed to frown, then almost smile. Julia wondered what he was thinking. Could he possibly know about her and Art? No, they had been very careful to watch everything they did and said while they had been here. She finally looked up at him and smiled, "Well, Papa. What do you want to do?"

"Well, you're right. It is difficult to let Jimmy go way up there so far away. But he is crazy about you, Jule. I just didn't know you were so wild about him. All

I remember is your fussing at him all the time and calling him names. What changed you?" He was looking very straight at her, watching her expressions closely. She didn't want to cry, and she didn't want to let her anger flow out of her in words. At least, not until Papa gave Jimmy to her. She did the best she could to keep her voice from wavering as she answered.

"I guess I really didn't think I loved him until I left. That has only been four weeks, and I found out I missed him so much I couldn't stand it. There's just the two of us now, and we're all we have. You can make another life for yourself with another family." She motioned toward the house slightly, and kept talking. "If you will give me legal custody of Jimmy, then there will be no trouble. Of course, I'm just eighteen, I know, but I have a good job, and Mr. Runyon thinks I'll be promoted soon to a better-paying job. I can make arrangements for him to go to school and everything. But, Papa, I won't do it unless you give me legal custody on paper. I don't want to do all the things necessary and get used to him, then you change your mind and take him back. I won't do that." She held her breath. She had never told Papa off in that way before. She could see Lila through the screen door. She knew Papa knew Lila was there, too, and he seemed nervous at her listening. He turned his back to the house, probably so his voice wouldn't travel toward the house, Julia thought.

"I don't think I can give you legal custody of him because you're just eighteen. Am I right?" He turned toward Art to ask him.

"I think you're right. But if you would like, you can make a stipulation that Jimmy will be in Julia's care and under my supervision until she is of age. I think my brother-in-law can help you draw up the necessary papers. You know she isn't trying to take Jimmy away from you. She just wants to be sure that he isn't swapped around to too many places which could happen if you decided in a few months to take him back. Then if you should just remarry, he would have another adjustment to make. It isn't good for a boy of ten to be moved around. I think if he were with Julia and felt secure there, this would be the best thing for him. I'll help her, and my wife will be delighted to give a hand."

"Alright, you tell me where to go to have the papers drawn up. Jule, I want you to know I'm not deserting. I'll send you money to take care of his expenses. I'm going to take a new job, traveling job. I may get up to Dallas sometimes. I'll drop in to see you."

"If you plan to come see us, you call first. I'm sorry, Papa, but you don't just have a place to sleep when you come to town. I have my own life and my own friends, and Jimmy will have his, too. We will be busy doing things together. I do not want you coming to the door at all hours or at unexpected times. I think I have the right to ask you to call, don't you? Would you want us to drop in on you just anytime?" She saw him look toward the house and drop his head. She knew she had struck a point with him.

"Agreed. I'll call you if I plan on visiting. Call me at this number when you get things set up for me to sign." He wrote a number down on the back of a slip up paper, which she found later was a sales slip for a dress. She wondered if it were for Mama or Lila. Oh well, never mind. She had gotten him to agree to let Jimmy come with her for good, and that was the important thing now. When they were safely far enough away from the house, Art turned down a small road toward the river, then stopped the car.

CHAPTER XI

The Transition

"Well, little one, that's what you wanted, wasn't it? You know our lives are going to have to be different now, don't you?"

"Yes, I've thought a lot about that. I can't thank you enough ever for helping me with Papa and Jimmy and everything. I know our lives will be different. We won't have an apartment to ourselves anymore. And we mustn't ever let Jimmy know about us. It's going to be so hard to get used to, looking after someone. I used to take care of him alright, but Mama made me do it then. Oh Art, do you think I can do it?"

"Of course, you can. You've got a level head on those shoulders. And you know I'm going to help you. There is one thing you've got to do, thought. You've got to meet Chris. We are going to make Jimmy see that both my wife and I like you both. It isn't going to be easy, either, but if we're smart as we've been so far, we can pull it off and it'll be better than ever."

This was something that Julia hadn't counted on. Meeting Art's wife, Chris, was the farthest thing from her mind right now. She knew Art was right, though. It would be nice for Jimmy, and nice for her, too. Well, first things first, and right now, the first thing was to go home and tell Jimmy and get his things packed. Art could see his brother-in-law about the papers. Suddenly, she had a horrible thought. What about Greg? What would she tell him? She knew Greg did love her. After all, he had driven down after her to give her the news. He had been over the next day, too, the day of the funeral but hadn't said much. She had the feeling he knew about her and Art. Well, what if he did? She had told Greg before more than once that he didn't own her. She had the right to do as he pleased, and she'd tell him so if she had to. Jimmy liked Greg a lot and would miss him. She would have to try very hard to make Jimmy happy, if for no other reason than for Mama's memory. Poor Mama. If she had only known Julia loved her and would take care of Jimmy, maybe the shock wouldn't have been great. Well, that was all in the past. She had too much to think about now to dwell on the past. As they drove on the hill toward the house, she saw Greg waiting in his car. Jimmy was much more pleased to see him than she was.

"When you get the papers finalized, call me here. I'll have to be there, I know, but I want to come after Papa leaves." She noticed a catch in her voice. After all, the events of the past three days had just about drained all the emotions out of her, and she felt she was going to break up. She held onto, and he noticed tears in her eyes.

"It'll all be alright, honey. Please don't let us down now. You've held up so wonderfully. It'll be just one more day, we'll be on our way to Dallas."

One more day. If it was like the past three, she didn't know if she could stand it or not. As Art drove away, she felt lonely and alone. She decided she had always felt like alone, even when she had lived at home with Mama and Papa and Jimmy. Why had she felt this way? Now she knew Jimmy loved her, and Mama loved her, too. She knew now why Mama had been so irritable and yelled at her sometimes. Mrs. Middleton had told her that Mama had been sick for a long time, almost since Jimmy was born, but Mama didn't want Julia to know. Mama had made her promise not to tell anyone, not even Papa. Mama didn't want Papa to come back to her because of pity, so only she and Mrs. Middleton and the doctor knew about Mama's condition, Julia felt ashamed when she heard about it. If she had only known, she could have been of more help and comfort to Mama, and she wouldn't have been so hateful about helping with Jimmy and the housework. Maybe she wouldn't have felt so alone if she had been a part of the secret.

"Hi, Greg. I'm going to Dallas to live with Jule, and I'm going to school just two blocks from the apartment." Greg just looked at him in amazement for a moment, then he looked at Julia as he turned his head in a questioning gaze.

"He's right. Jimmy, go in the house and start getting your things together. Out them all out on your bed and I'll be in to help you pack them." Then, turning to Greg, she crossed her fingers and began explaining. "Papa has given me legal custody of him. After all, he doesn't want him around with his new interests, or rather his same old interests. Did you know about Lila?"

"Yes, I've known for a long time. I heard my folks talking about it a couple of years ago. I guess it's common knowledge to almost everybody."

"Well, that's nice. It wasn't common knowledge to me. I didn't know until Mrs. Middleton told me two days ago. You might have told me. After all, it did concern me and Mama and Jimmy!" She flew at him with rage now. To think that he had known for two years and hadn't even hinted her of such a thing.

"What would you have done? He very seldom stayed at home, anyway. He paid the bills, and kept you and your mother a car to drive. What could you have done except make a scene and maybe spoil your chance to graduate? What?"

She realized Greg was right in one way. She couldn't have done anything but make a scene, and she surely would have done that. With Mama sick, things would have been pretty bad if Papa had just left. For the first time since she realized that Greg was a smart, sensible boy. He was always looking out for her best interest, and he did like Mama and Jimmy.

"I'm sorry. I guess, you're right. I couldn't have done anything. The only thing I could have done, if

I had been mature enough to realize it, would have been to help Mama more, and I think it would have been to help Mama more, and I think it would have made me feel closer to her and Jimmy, too. When I think of her keeping her illness from me and keeper her trouble with Papa from me, oh Greg…I could have been so much pleasure and help to Mama." She leaned her head on Greg's shoulder. He tried to ease her mind by telling her that Mama didn't want her to know about all the trouble. All she wanted was for her children to live normal happy lives. Greg kissed her forehead as he held her. She looked up into his face, tears streaming down her cheeks, and tried to smile. He leaned down and kissed her, softly and tenderly, then held her and whispered in her ear. "I love you, Jule. Don't go away again. Stay here and marry me. I love you."

She leaned back and looked squarely at Greg. He had tears in his eyes and had the look of love that she had seen in movies when someone handsome was asking some beautiful leading lady to share his life forever. This was a more mature Greg than the one who had asked her to marry him in the boat when they were fifteen. Now he held her with a strength and passion that she could feel close to her body. She didn't like this. It was disconcerting, to say the least. She only loved Art and he was going to be with her forever; that is, all the times he could be away from Chris.

"Greg, I want to thank you for what you've meant to me during all this horrible time. I know

Jimmy has really appreciated our friendship and kindness, too. You've always been like a brother to me. I love you like that, and that's all. I'm in love with someone else."

She realized as soon as she said it that she shouldn't have. He pushed her away a little with a strong stiff arm and held her shoulders with fingers that were gripping into her arm.

"Who could you be in love with? You've only been gone four weeks, and that's not long enough to be in love with anyone. What have you been doing while you've been in Dallas?"

She felt a blush to her cheeks when he looked deep into her eyes with sort of penetrating look, like he could search her very soul and root out the truth.

"I told you one time that I'd go with whomever I wanted and do whatever I wanted, do you remember that?"

"Yes, I remember that. That time, I asked you to marry me, too. You may be sorry, Jule. I may not ever ask you again. Whoever that it is that you think you're in love with, I just hope you have the good sense not to fall for him and let yourself get pregnant or do some such stupid thing like that. I would hate to see your life spoiled and Jimmy's, too. I really do love you and want to take care of you and Jimmy. After all, I have a pretty good job down here. Maybe it's not as exciting as Dallas, but sometimes love can make for a lot. You'd better remember that."

As he stalked off to his car and got in and burned off to get out of there fast, she had a feeling of loneliness that she couldn't explain. As if part of her life had ended this day. First, she had lost Mama, and now Greg.

"I'm ready, Jule." Jimmy came running out of the house and threw himself around her waist. "Let's get packed and go. I can't wait to get to Dallas. Is it exciting, Jule?"

"Yes. It's exciting and so different from here. You can hear cars all day and night in front in the street. Somebody is always going somewhere. There are stores within walking distance in practically every direction. There's a park just two blocks over with a swimming pool and lots of trees and swings and slides and all that stuff. There's a movie just four blocks from our apartment."

Our apartment. She thought about how it had been hers and Art's apartment. Now there was Jimmy. Things were certainly going to change. They would end up at motels again if Jimmy didn't have something going on. She suddenly couldn't wait for Art to be back to pick them up and be on the way out of this place. All she could think of this place was how sad she had been here and how lonely. By tomorrow, she'd be back at her job and see Art and go with him and he'd love her and he'd help her with Jimmy and it would all be fine. She was absolutely sure of that. Tomorrow, her life would start over again.

CHAPTER XII

SETTLING DOWN TO LIFE

As the weeks rocked along, Jimmy was used to the playground and meeting friends, while her job got more demanding. She now had to work partly for Art and partly for Lew, the attorney for the company. She found herself working overtime several days each week, and when she would get home and fix Jimmy and herself a bite to eat, she was so tired that sometimes she'd just get ready for bed. It was a demanding life, and worst of all, she didn't get to see Art alone as much as she would have liked.

As hard as she tried, she couldn't help letting a little bit of disappointment creep in her at times when she talked to Jimmy about their lives together. She had promised herself Jimmy would never know about her and Art. He was so happy when they would go over to see Chris, whether Art was there or not. Chris often invited them to swim or just visit in the backyard. The times Art was there, they acted just like employer and employee, and kept it nice and fatherly, daughterly. It was hard, but it had to be that way.

When Jimmy started school in the fall, it meant days alone, and sometimes she would go into the office late with various excuses, just so Art could come to the apartment after Jimmy left for school. They knew they couldn't do that too much without causing problems in the office. One day while Julia was in Lew's office, Art dropped in as if about a file and casually brought up the subject of Julia's overtime.

"You know, Lew, I've been thinking that we're working this poor girl too many hours."

Lew looked at her and at Art, thought a while, and asked Art, "What did you have in mind?"

"Well, I've been thinking that since we obviously need her for bids and reports, reservations, etc. why couldn't she come in two days a week at 1:00 p.m. and stay till 9:00 p.m. and clean up all the things that Polly can't get done before 5:00 p.m. and that way, we'll have someone in the office from 8:00-9:00 p.m., and yet neither of them will have work over." Julia's heart fairly jumped. She knew why Art was suggesting this. They had tried to think of some way to have more time together, and this was the way. She crossed her fingers and waited for Lew's response.

"Well, by golly! You know, I think you have a point there. She has been pushing it, I know, coming in at 8:00 a.m. and not going home till 7:00 or 8:00 p.m. Hasn't been easy, has it, Julia?"

"Well, to tell you the truth, wand the added responsibilities here and the extra work, sometimes

I'm so tired when I get home and I just eat and go to bed. That would be great if I could work it that way. I don't mind working if I'm needed. You both know that, but I really don't have the time at home even to wash clothes or clean house anymore."

"Then, it's settled. Julia, start coming in at least two days at 1:00 p.m. you decide which days you'd like and get together with Polly on which days are the heaviest and just let us know what your schedule is. I'll be glad to know that you're here certain evenings because when I'm at auctions or markets, sometimes I need some information here and don't have anyone to give it to me." With that, Art left for his office with a feeling of accomplishment. Julia breathed a sigh of relief and went to talk to Polly.

Another problem solved by Art, she thought to herself, as she went down the hallway to the office she shared with Polly.

Soon, it was Christmas and the holidays. Jimmy was out of school for two weeks and she had to think of how to handle all the time off. Chris suggested that Jimmy could stay with her a few days if it would help Julia, and she thought it was a wonderful idea.

When she told Art, he literally jumped with joy. They could have the apartment all to themselves for a while. They would have to be really careful to not let anything slip so either Chris or Jimmy would be suspicious. The first full week off, Art got the idea that he and Chris would take both of them out for dinner.

That wat, Jimmy and Julia could be together, and they would all have a wonderful time. They all went to a local pizza place with games and videos, and all of them really had a wonderful time. There were many times like that, and many time Art would go over to the apartment after Jimmy left for school on the days that Julia was to go in at 1:00 p.m. This helped her to feel better about her life and not be so lonely.

One day, she picked up the phone and it was Greg. She found herself glad to hear from him. He told her all about what he had been doing since he had seen her. He had been Pastor Ashley with the youth camp and Bible school. He told her what a good time he had; add that he wished Jimmy had been there, too. He said he would have had such a great time. Julia said he probably would have because Jimmy liked Greg so much.

Greg was quiet for a minute, and then said, "Jule, I want you to be the first person to know I have surrendered to be a youth pastor. I felt God had been telling me something for a long time, and when I talked to Pastor Ashely, he asked me if I thought God was asking me to surrender to the ministry. We prayed about it and I knew that's what God wanted me to do."

Julia didn't quite know what to say, but she heard the joy in his voice and knew this was a decision that made him happy. She finally said, "Greg, I am so happy for you. I can tell by your voice that this decision wasn't reached lightly, and I think all the youth will be so blessed to have you."

"Julia, I am going to School of Divinity next month. It is about sixty miles from you. Maybe I can see you some time."

She said they would be so glad to see him and to just let them know what weekend he would be able to drive over. She told him how busy she was with her work, and how Chris and Art have helped her with Jimmy and how he loved school and all the new friends, too. She told him she didn't know how smart Jimmy was. He's making all A's and B's. Greg said he always knew how smart Jimmy was if he had just been given a chance. He also said how he had always known how much Jimmy had loved her and he's so glad they're together now.

When she hung the phone up, she just sat there a while. Greg a youth pastor. She knew he would be a good one, and everyone who comes in contact with him would be better off for having met him.

When she saw Art. She told him about Greg's call. He waited a minute to answer her and then said, "I tell you one thing. That boy has put a great deal of thought and prayer into this, and I just hope all turns out the way he wants it to."

Everything was going pretty well. Jimmy was on the baseball team. Art loved to go to the games. They all went to the ones that were om the weekend. They all had a great time together. Julia was now nineteen and thought of what was going to happen when Jimmy graduated. That was a long time off, but nevertheless, she had already been thinking about it.

One day, Ray Wheatley stopped by her desk and asked her if she's happy with her job. Julia told him "Absolutely, yes." She wondered if he was thinking about putting her somewhere else. Her heart nearly stopped when she thought he might be wanting her to go to another office. He asked her to come to his office in about thirty minutes. She was so nervous she could hardly type. She went into the office and Art was there, too. Her heart nearly stopped.

He started the conversation with "Art, you've been sales manager for over ten years. The company has grown by nearly fifty since you took over. I've been wondering, do you think you could use an assistant sales manager?" Art said he had thinking the same lately. Ray looked at Julia and said, "Julia, do you think you could hold down the position of assistant sales manager?"

She looked at Art and he had a smile on his face, so she knew he had already talked to Ray about this. "You know I can't travel because I have my little brother with me."

"We've already thought about that. Art's wife has said that if there is ever a time like at conventions, she would be happy to have someone around when Art is gone sometimes."

Her heart sped up. She knew Art had thought this all out and she would be happy to accompany him to the conventions with everyone's blessing. How wonderful that would be. They would have five whole days and nights to be together! She said, "Yes, then I would be happy to take the position. Assistant sales manager sounds great."

The next week, the notices went out and everyone knew she was the Assistant sales manager. She moved into an office right beside Art's, and she just thought she had never been so happy. Polly would now help her, as well as Art. She didn't know how that would go, but she'd give it a try.

The first convention came in January. They had all had a great Christmas and now were getting ready for the convention. Her heart was pumping when she heard that their tickets were in.

Jimmy moved over to Chris's house on Sunday before they left at 4:00 p.m. they drove to the airport. She had never flown. She told Art, and he told her not to worry because he wasn't going to let her go the whole flight. She looked at him smiled. She felt perfectly safe now. The three-hour flight was simply fabulous. She had, of course, seen the Gulf of Mexico but she had never seen the ocean. She got the first glimpse of Los Angeles and the Pacific Ocean, and it was just breathtaking. She thought of all those times sitting by the river at home and how she loved the water. This was magnificent!

When they arrived, they got the taxi to the Hotel and checked in. Of course, each in their own room with an adjoining door. He had already taken care of this himself. He didn't Polly to know about the adjoining door. As soon as they got there, they checked in, went to their rooms, then went to the adjoining door and opened it. They fell into each other's arms. They didn't care which room they went to but it ended up in Julia's. this was like the first time had made love in the motel. They just held one another for a long time, and finally made love.

They freshened up and then went downstairs to the restaurant. He said he was just famished. She said she was, too. She had been so excited she couldn't eat anything since yesterday. It was a wonder she didn't pass out.

They were having a great meal when everything just went to pot. One of the other company came over and said hello, and Art introduced them, and the other man said, "Holy Toledo, your wife is letting you come here with this ravishing redhead?"

Art was so angry with him that he said they really didn't have time to kill because they have to go over strategies and sales. The man got the hint and said good-bye and left. Art looked at Julie and said, "I'm sorry, honey. I guess, I just forgot there were people like that in the industry."

The next day, they arrived on the convention floor at 8:00 a.m. but came from opposite doors. This would throw them off, maybe. The convention was great. Very harrowing work. Memory is the most important thing you can have at a place like this. They had their files to back them up, but they had to know who bought what the time before, who was sales manager, who got the awards, etc. Fortunately, Julia had a good memory and had pored over with a fine-toothed comb. She was so proud when she was able to answer Art's questions. He looked pleased, too.

Soon, it was over and they were on their way to a restaurant. He decided to go to one a couple of blocks away so maybe they wouldn't run into anyone from the convention. They didn't. It was so great to be alone and be able to look at each other like they wanted to.

The whole five days were like a dream. Working with Art, sleeping with him, eating with him. She loved conventions and wanted another one soon.

When they got back and got the car and drove his house to get to Jimmy, she was all wound up. She hugged Jimmy and Chris, and told them all about the deals she had helped close. She was so wound up that no one else could get in a word. Art looked at Chris and told her she had been that way all back on the plane and he hadn't even got to sleep. She thought that would stop any thoughts from happening. She thought she pulled it off pretty good.

Their lives kept on pretty smoothly till the end of the school year. Jimmy would now go into the high school next year. He still played baseball, and Art went when he could. She was getting ready for another convention and wrapped in sales deals and promotions. She heard from Greg every few weeks. He was happy doing what he was and told her he had a workshop in the high church in Dallas coming up. He asked if she and Jimmy would like to come out to one of the Sunday sessions. She asked Jimmy, and he was all for it. He had missed Greg. He thought it would be a good chance to tell him what all he had been doing, too.

They got dressed and took a taxi to the church to meet Greg. When she saw him, he hugged her and Jimmy and was so glad to see them. They talked about fifteen minutes before they went in to the auditorium. There were hundreds of people there; more than half it looked like were the youth. He took them to a seat he had saved for them, and then he joined the group on the podium. She thought he looked good up there. He looked poised, happy, and at ease. Yes, he really looked like this is what he loved to do.

Greg drove them back home after dinner. He wanted to be with them as long as he could. Julia had to admit that she was proud of what Greg is doing. He really made a difference in those kid's lives.

Art dropped a truth bomb on her the next week. He said he and Chris were going on a vacation up to the East Coast. He said he wanted to go for a while, and now that she could shoulder some of the responsibilities of the job, they thought they'd go for a week. He told Julia he'd miss her, but she's be so busy with all the things she had to do she wouldn't have time to miss him.

CHAPTER XIII

Learning to Face Loss Again

That week was long and lonely. She and Jimmy went to the movies one night and went out to eat another night. That made the week go a little faster. On Thursday morning when she went to work, she was met at the door by Ray Wheaton. He had a solemn look and it scared her. He took her into his office, had her sit down and, and told her he had some bad news. She caught her breath and knew it was something bad. He told her that the night before, there had been a bad accident, and Art and Chris were killed instantly. She felt the blood draining from her head, and she keeled over in the chair. Ray called for help, and Polly came in and wiped her face with a cold wet towel. She came to and couldn't say anything. She just looked straight ahead.

When she thought about it, she almost cried. She had to watch out and not start crying. She just swallowed and got up and she said she had to go home and tell Jimmy because he loved them so much. She said this was just like losing Mama all over again.

When she got home, she told Jimmy and they both held one another and cried just like they had three years ago when Mama died.

She couldn't believe it had only been three years. They had been through so much, how could they get through so much, how could they get through this? The first thing she thought of was to call Greg. He just couldn't believe it and said he'd come right over. He was there in an hour. He must have speeded a lot. He just held her and Jimmy as they cried till they were exhausted, they all wiped their eyes and started talking about the things that needed to get done.

She found out from Ray that Art and Chris had signed papers to be cremated. That meant that they would send their ashes here for a memorial service. The company would take care of all of that.

Julia thought to herself that she didn't know if she could sit through a service looking at an URN not knowing Art was gone. She started to cry and knew she had to get control of herself, if for no other reason than for Jimmy.

Greg stayed with them and took them out to dinner so they could get their minds off everything that had happened. They found themselves comparing this to when their Mama had died. Greg said he would be glad to help with everything that he could. He thought of a great deal of Art, too. Art had called him not long ago to ask how Greg thought Julia and Jimmy were getting along. They talked about Greg's new life, too, as youth minister. Art had told him he was proud of him for following the road he had started. Art said he thought Greg would make a great youth minister, and maybe a great minister. Greg told him he hadn't even thought along those lines, but if asked to do it he would give it some fervent prayer and thought. When he told Julia about the call, she just smiled and thought about what Art was thinking. He had told her that he really liked Greg, and told her to remember what he told her. He told her that Greg was in love with her. He said, "I told you that when your mother died, remember?" She just smiled.

The next day, she called Ray at the office to ask what were the plans. She hadn't gone in today because she just didn't know if she could work and go in the office beside Art's office. In fact, she didn't know if she could walk there at all with all the memories. Ray told her he wanted her to stay home on an extended time off until they worked out some problems. There was the convention coming up and something would have to be done by that time. She talked to Greg about it. He said he would have to get back to work if she wanted to stay in Dallas. She told him that she definitely wanted to stay. After all, Jimmy had his school, his friends, his ball team, and she loved the apartment and had loved working. She didn't know how that would all work out. Greg said God would help all to work out right.

The next morning, Ray called Julia and she said she and Jimmy and Greg needed to come to the office around 1:00 p.m. He told her that Art's sister, Jenny, and her husband, needed them there, too. She told him that they would be there. When she told Greg and Jimmy about the call, they just wondered what was going on but said they'd go.

When they arrived, she saw Jenny and recognized her from times when she and Greg and James had all graduated three years ago. She remembered that was the day she met Art. She quickly thought about holding Art's hand and looking into those dark eyes. She caught her breath and went over to hug Jenny and tell her how sorry she was for her loss. She introduced them to Jimmy, and then Bob said, "Oh yes, we've heard a lot about this young man. Art and Chris couldn't say enough about him and his sister, Julia. I want you to know that you made their lives easier because you helped fill the giant hole in their hearts from the loss of their son. They didn't start thinking about you instead of their son, but it made them easier to think about him. We want to thank you for both of that. In fact, they came by to see us the day they started on their trip. They had me fix some legal papers for them they said if anything happened to them, they wanted to make sure all of you were taken care of." Julia looked at Jimmy and Greg with a quizzical look. She didn't know what was coming.

Bob told them that when they were there, they had set up trust accounts for all of them and their son, James. They had opened accounts for all four of them and put $10,000.00 in each of their accounts. They were in their names with Art as guardian. Jimmy's was to be used as a college account. He could draw out when he began college and use it the full years if there was enough, and then when he got out of college he could use it for whatever he wanted. There was supposed to be $10,000.00 put in each account each year, but of course that all stopped. Greg's was to be used by him in his youth ministry as he saw fit. He could use it for camp, schools, scholarships, or whatever he wanted to do God's work. Julia's was to be used by her to help take care of her and Jimmy and their needs. James was to be used for his college and continuing on to get his master's like he had planned to do. He had told Art that he wanted to get a master's in teaching and planned to go on for a doctorate if he could manage the finances.

Then, Bob told them that both Art and Chris had made out new wills that day. In the wills, of course, each one left everything to the other one. They also stipulated that if they should both die together, their money was to be given out this way: Bob was to sell the house and put all the money in an account to be divided this way: $250,000.00 was to go to each of the four of them. All the cars were to be given to Julia for her and Jimmy. Since Art's convertible was totaled, that insurance check would go to Julia to buy her a new car. The smaller one that Chris drove was to be Jimmy's when he came of age. What was left is to go to Jenny. Art said he would always treasure the memories of her when they were growing up.

Jenny asked Julia and Jimmy if they had anything in the house they would like, or if some of their things were in it. She said she knew they spent a lot of their time over there. She also asked Julia if there was anything in the house that she would like for hers. She said Chris had told her that all her jewels were to go to Julia. She said she hadn't been blessed with a daughter but Julia was the closest thing to a daughter she had. Julia told Jenny that there was a painting that she had loved and teased Chris that she should bequeath it to her! She also had a lamp in *her room* where she stayed when she stayed over that she liked. Jenny told her to come over that afternoon and pick up the painting, lamp, and all Chris's jewels. Julia couldn't stand it anymore. She just broke down and Greg came over and put his arm around her. She thought how reassuring that felt.

Ray came in and told them that the company had gotten together with their public relations manager and decided that the memorial service for Art and Chris would be held the following Saturday at the Memorial Park at one of the huge cemeteries, and their ashes would be interred in the huge vault.

Well, after Saturday, it would all be over. She told herself she had to stay solid for Jimmy and she would. Greg, of course, would take them to the memorial. She thought again at how good it felt for him to put his arm around her. She thought about Greg a lot that night and the next day. She wondered if Art had had a premonition that something might happen to him and that's why he told her that Greg loved her. Was he getting ready to accept the loss and move on? Surely, he couldn't have foreseen what was going to happen. Greg had told her that he felt Art would be in heaven. He said they had had some private conversations about God. That's all he would say, though. He said private conversations are sacred and not to be talked about. In her heart, she hoped that Chris would forgive her and that God would, too. She asked God's forgiveness, and then went to sleep.

They got up at 8:00 a.m. on Saturday and got dressed after eating a little breakfast. Neither of them was hungry, but they knew it would be a hard day and they should put something in their stomach.

When it was over, Greg took them out for dinner and they talked about what their lives looked like. They finally discussed they money that Art and Chris had left them. Now Jimmy would have his college paid for and she could get her a good car. She also intended to invest some of the money in some good plans. She would talk to the financial advisor at work.

Their lives started to smooth out and they went to school games with Jimmy, went out to eat, went to movies and plays at the open-air theatre. She found she looked forward to Greg's calls and his visits. Jimmy was making all A's and loved school. She thought that had a lot to do with Greg. They had gone over to church with Greg several time, and Jimmy had gone on a youth retreat with Greg. He had such a wonderful time and couldn't stop talking about it and how great Greg was.

CHAPTER XIV

Love Conquers All

She heard the minister saying, "What God hath joined together, let no man put asunder. I now pronounce you man and wife."

She now was Greg's wife and she felt absolutely fabulous. She realized that for years she had loved Greg but just wouldn't admit it to herself. He was her rock and she had not admitted it. She looked at Jimmy standing there in his tuxedo, beaming. He said now his world was just about as good as it could get. Greg told him to just wait until he fell head over heels for some girl and he'd see that it could topsy-turvy again. We all had a good laugh. We went down the aisle and out and said our goodbyes to everyone and got into the car. Greg grabbed me and held me so tight and said, "I've loved you practically all my life, but I've never loved you as much as I love you right now."

About the Author

D.L smith is eighty-six years old and has met thousands of people in those years. She is a businesswoman and has been in several countries. She is a *people person* and has a great memory for details. Many people in her books are compilations of several people she has known in her lifetime.

CPSIA information can be obtained
at www.ICGtesting.com
Printed in the USA
LVHW010345201021
700870LV00003B/84

9 781648 955969